# Thanksgiving Day

# THANKSGIVING DAY

STORY BY **Anne Rockwell**    PICTURES BY **Lizzy Rockwell**

## SCHOLASTIC INC.

New York   Toronto   London   Auckland   Sydney
Mexico City   New Delhi   Hong Kong

ISBN 0-439-21133-6

Text copyright © 1999 by Anne Rockwell. Illustrations copyright © 1999 by Lizzy Rockwell. All rights reserved. Published by Scholastic Inc., 555 Broadway, New York, NY 10012, by arrangement with HarperCollins Publishers. SCHOLASTIC and associated logos are trademarks and/or registered trademarks of Scholastic Inc.

12 11 10 9 8 7 6 5 4 3 2 1                    0 1 2 3 4 5/0

Printed in the U.S.A.                                  09

First Scholastic printing, November 2000

*For Nicholas and Nigel,*
*and their Nonna Phyllis*
*—A.R. & L.R.*

Some historians believe the first Thanksgiving was celebrated in the Jamestown Colony, though it has traditionally been placed in Massachusetts. For a long while, people thought that landing on Plymouth Rock was legend, but recent evidence indicates that this may truly have been the spot where the Pilgrims from the Mayflower *first set foot.* —A.R.

Special thanks to the curators and interpreters at Plimoth Plantation and to the preservationists at the Cape Cod National Seashore.
The children's costumes in this book were inspired by those made by the students at New Lebanon Elementary School, Greenwich, Connecticut. —L.R.

Do you know why we celebrate Thanksgiving?
Do you know why we always eat turkey, corn bread,
and cranberry sauce on Thanksgiving Day?
I do. I learned why in school.

Our teacher, Mrs. Madoff,
read us the story of
the first Thanksgiving.
I like that story.

We learned about the Wampanoag people
who were already in this land,

and the Pilgrims who came
across the sea from England.

Pilgrim men wore tall black hats
with silver buckles
and Pilgrim women wore white caps.

Wampanoag people wore leather headbands
with feathers in them.

After the story,
we put on a play.
I went first.
I was the ship
called the *Mayflower.*
I told how
I was thankful that
I tossed and rolled,
and tossed
and rolled
some more,
but didn't sink
in the big waves
far out at sea.

Evan was a Wampanoag named Samoset.
He was thankful for all the wild turkeys
that lived in the land
his people called Massachusetts.
He told how one day he saw
the *Mayflower* sailing toward his land.

Sarah told how all the Pilgrims were thankful
when they finally reached land.
They named a big rock Plymouth Rock,
after the place they came from in England.
They saw lots of wild cranberries growing.
"That's why we eat cranberry sauce
at Thanksgiving," Sarah said.

Nicholas told how he was thankful
for forests full of trees.
The Pilgrims chopped them down
to build warm houses.

Pablo was Squanto.
He was thankful
that all the kernels of corn
the Wampanoag people planted
sprouted and grew
tall and green.

Sam was thankful
   that Squanto told him
      wild turkeys were good to eat
       and taught him how to hunt them.
       The Pilgrims had never seen
       a wild turkey in England.
       They'd never tasted one, either.
       It was delicious!

Michiko was thankful
that she and all the other Pilgrims
were greeted kindly
by the Wampanoag people,
who shared the land with them.

Kate was thankful
that her new neighbors
were peaceful Pilgrims
looking for a new land
to live in,
and not mean people
looking for someone
to fight with.

Jessica was thankful
that the beautiful land
of Massachusetts
had enough good things
for everyone.

Eveline was Chief Massasoit.
She told how the Wampanoag and Pilgrim people
shared their harvest feast one autumn day.

That was the first Thanksgiving!

It's a story we'll never forget.
It's something we celebrate every year.

Today is our Thanksgiving holiday.
We don't go to school or work today.

Instead we celebrate and are thankful at home.
We eat turkey, corn bread, and cranberry sauce.

We invite our family, friends, and neighbors
to share our feast,
just as the Pilgrims and Wampanoag people did.